THE CREATIVE COOK

Aromatic

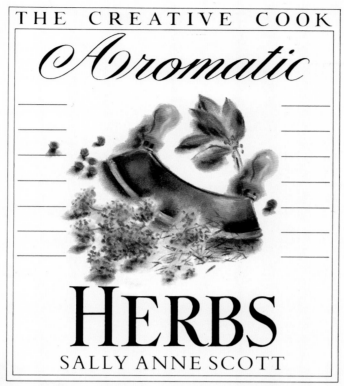

HERBS

SALLY ANNE SCOTT

FOREWORD BY GERALDENE HOLT

PHOTOGRAPHY BY PIA TRYDE

CONRAN OCTOPUS

To David with thanks for his inspiration in and
out of the kitchen.

Please note the following:

Quantities given in all the recipes serve 4 people unless otherwise stated.

Spoon measurements are level unless otherwise stated.

Metric and imperial measures are both given, use one or the other as the two are not interchangeable.

Flour used is plain white flour, unless otherwise specified.

Preparation of ingredients, such as the cleaning, trimming and peeling of vegetables and fruit, is presumed and the text only refers to any aspect of this if unusual, such as onions used unpeeled etc.

Citrus fruit is generally coated in a layer of preservative wax. For this reason, whenever a recipe uses the rind of oranges, lemons or limes the text specifies unwaxed fruit. If organic uncoated fruit is not available, scrub the fruit vigorously in hot soapy water, rinse well and pat dry.

Eggs used are size 3 (65 g/2¼ oz) unless otherwise specified. The Government recommends that eggs not be consumed raw, and people most at risk, such as children, old people, invalids and pregnant women, should not eat them lightly cooked. This book includes recipes with raw and lightly cooked eggs, which should not be eaten by the above categories. These recipes are marked by a * in the text. Once prepared, these dishes should be kept refrigerated and used promptly.

Editorial Direction: Lewis Esson Publishing
Art Director: Mary Evans
Design: Sue Storey
Illustrations: Alison Barratt
Food for Photography: Meg Jansz
Styling: Jane Newdick
Editorial Assistant: Penny David
Production: Jill Macey

First published in 1992 by
Conran Octopus Limited,
37 Shelton Street, London WC2H 9HN

This new edition published in 1993 by
Conran Octopus Limited.

British Library Cataloguing in Publication Data
A catalogue record for this book is available from the British Library

ISBN 1-85029-438-0

Typeset by Hunters Armley Ltd
Printed and bound in Hong Kong.

CONTENTS

FOREWORD

For me, few cooking ingredients give such profound pleasure as fresh herbs. The intense aroma of chopped mint leaves added to a lemon sauce or of bright green sweet basil torn into shreds for a tomato salad is both alluring and appetizing. I also never fail to be surprised by the transformation in the flavour of a dish by the addition of just a sprig of, say, tarragon or rosemary. The right herb not only complements the flavour of other ingredients in cooking but reveals their true flavour.

Herbs have long been part of our culinary history. Some, such as sorrel and sweet cicely, are native wild plants. Others, like chives and thyme, were introduced into Britain by the Romans and continued to thrive in the monastic herb gardens that survived until the time of Henry VIII. Since the Reformation, herbs have been grown in every part of our country in both large and small gardens. Even today, no self-respecting cook's garden is cultivated without, at least, a clump of parsley and a patch of mint.

Yet we often remain wary of utilizing to the full these important plants. Cooks are sometimes concerned that the flavour of a herb will overwhelm or spoil a dish. If you are hesitant about cooking with herbs add just a small amount – such as a lovage or bay leaf – to a home-made soup or stew. Then gradually experiment with other kinds; stir chopped dill into a sauce for salmon or some coriander leaves into a dish of cooked potatoes. Add small sprigs of herbs like rocket, chervil and ginger mint to a salad. Finally progress to those characterful sauces like Genoese *pesto* and savoury Montpellier butter that depend upon a good handful of herbs for their identity and richness.

So familiar are some of the accustomed herbal associations that cooks can be reluctant to develop new ideas. Take, for instance, the handsome felty-leaved sage; now sage is such an excellent herb in its well-known role (combined with onion and breadcrumbs) in a stuffing for poultry, that we easily forget that chopped fresh sage is also a fine herb for adding to cheese dishes or to a sauce for pasta, or for flavouring breads or scones.

Although in European cookery it is quite common to add herbs to savoury dishes, it is worth remembering that in English cooking of the time of Elizabeth I sweet dishes too were flavoured with aromatic herbs. I think of the heavenly fragrance of the rose-scented geranium or mauve lavender blossoms, or the bewitching flavours of lemon verbena, elderflower and pineapple sage, and how well they perfume cream, custards and water ices.

Once you have gained confidence in cooking with herbs, you will find that ideas dawn for your own delicious dishes. Your cooking will become more adventurous and lively as fresh herbs give dishes a uniquely satisfying and individual character that will be appreciated by both yourself and those for whom you cook.

GERALDENE HOLT

INTRODUCTION

*H*erbs have played an essential part in our lives for centuries. From their earliest instinctive use in primitive tribal magic, they came eventually to be systematically studied and dispensed by apothecaries and physicians, and grown in monastery gardens. John Gerard in his great *Herball* of 1597 described the supposed properties of over 1,100 types. Now in modern-day herbalism, homeopathy and aromatherapy, herbs have found renewed respect in all forms.

The culinary use of herbs has also been fairly continuous, although until recently in Britain – in the cities at least – we had become somewhat unadventurous, sticking only to a well-tried handful like parsley, sage and thyme. Now, however, we are thankfully rediscovering the exciting and delicious flavours of these wonderfully versatile plants and using them to enhance our food on a daily basis.

The proven medicinal qualities of herbs can also benefit us in many ways when incorporated regularly in our diets. Stronger flavoured herbs may be used as an alternative to ordinary seasonings and can thus help to cut down our salt intake. They may also help offset the possible blandness of low-fat and high-fibre dishes.

BUYING, GROWING AND PRESERVING HERBS

Most herbs sold commercially are preserved by drying. As a general rule, dried herbs are more potent than fresh. A good rule of thumb is to use three times as much fresh as dried.

It is now increasingly easy to buy fresh herbs all year round – either cut in small sachets or growing in tiny pots. It is, however, also very simple and fun to grow – and dry – your own. Space is not always vital, since many are very happy in window boxes, on balconies, in a tiny garden or even on the roof. Picking should always be on a sunny dry day, when the flowers are just about to appear, as this ensures the fullest flavours and retains most of the aromatic essential oils. Try not too bruise the leaves too much.

Drying can be done by tying the herbs in small bunches, then hanging them in a dust-free, light and airy space – warm, but out of direct sunlight. Herbs with seed heads, such as dill, fennel or coriander, should have small paper bags tied over them into which the seeds may be shaken. They will fall naturally, or may be gently rubbed to hasten the process.

Most herbs may also be frozen, although not all are suitable and I feel that there is at least a 20 per cent loss of flavour in most cases. Place the fresh herbs in cellophane bags or small plastic tubs. Small amounts may be chopped and frozen in ice cube trays for easily separable small quantities. Basil, marjoram, chives and parsley are the best survivors of this method of preservation, but remember that they will always lose their colour.

STORING AND PREPARING HERBS

Dried herbs should be kept in cool places well away from sunlight in order to preserve their essential oils – little glass jars in spice racks above the stove is exactly how *not* to store them! Buy them from stores with a rapid turnover and mark the date of purchase on the container, as their flavouring properties do not last much more than about 6 months.

Fresh herbs may either be kept in polythene bags in the salad drawer of the refrigerator or, if they have intact stalks, stand them like flowers in a vase or glass of water on a windowsill.

Preparation of herbs is usually fairly straightforward. Fresh leaves are usually finely chopped or snipped with scissors directly into a dish. Some, like basil, cooks prefer to bruise or tear rather than cut as this is held to preserve more of the oils. If in the habit of cutting large amounts of herbs, it is worth investing in a mezzaluna – a double-handled crescent-shaped knife – with a bowl curved to match the blade. Alternatively, a careful hand on the pulse of a food processor can cut down time and effort.

Seeds are usually lightly crushed in a mortar with a pestle before use or crushed to a powder in a spice or coffee grinder or in a food processor.

CHOOSING THE RIGHT HERB

After exhausting all the tried-and-tested classic combinations – like sage and onion, peas and mint, lamb and rosemary etc – many people are quite bewildered by the sheer diversity of choice and are reluctant to experiment with herbs for fear of making expensive mistakes. I hope the recipes in this book will provide some ideas of ways to go. Also note the herb use in favourite foreign food – lemon grass in Thai food, basil in pasta and pizza sauces etc – and take a lead from them. Don't forget to look at old recipe books for ideas – even Mrs Beeton included lemon thyme, marjoram, winter savory and basil in her basic 'herb powder for flavouring'.

Angelica *(Angelica archangelica)*
Stems are crystallized for cake decoration and for flavouring puddings and some soft white cheeses. Good stewed with tart-flavoured fruit.

Anise *(Pimpinella anisum)*
Pungent in flavour. Crushed seeds used in cakes, biscuits, fruit desserts, soup and fish dishes. Very good digestive properties. Leaves used with fruit.

Basil *(Ocimum basilicum)*
Extremely versatile with a warm spicy flavour, leaves are used to best effect with tomatoes, either shredded raw over salads or cooked in pasta sauces. The flavour also works well in dishes with garlic and wine and in creamy sauces. Several varieties with subtly different flavours, one lemon-scented.

Bay *(Laurus nobilis)*
One of the most used culinary herbs and an essential ingredient for bouquet garni, fresh or dried leaves work particularly well in stocks, casseroles, pâtés, game and poultry dishes and in pickling.

Bergamot *(Monarda didyma)*
Highly perfumed leaves good in small quantities for stuffings, salads and sweet dishes.

Borage *(Borago officinalis)*
Flowers crystallized for cake decoration, while leaves used in salads and stuffings and for fritters. Popular for refreshing summer fruit cups.

Caraway *(Carum carvi)*
Aromatic seeds crushed for flavouring cakes, biscuits, breads, cheese, cabbage, stews and salads.

Celery *(Apium graveolens)*
Leaves used in salads and soups and in poultry stuffings and fish sauces. Seeds used in pickling and to flavour stews and curried dishes. Ground and sold as celery salt, useful for low-sodium diets.

Chervil *(Anthriscus cerefolium)*
Delicately flavoured leaves are an ingredient of fines herbes. The flavour goes well in salads and dressings, with spring vegetables and in white fish and egg dishes. Good blood-cleansing properties.

Chives *(Allium schoenoprasum)*
Flower heads used for garnish. Delicate onion-flavoured leaves best used raw or lightly cooked especially as a garnish for soups, salads and egg dishes. Also for meat, fish, poultry and vegetable dishes and in cheese mixtures, dips and dressings.

Coriander *(Coriandrum sativum)*
Distinctive earthy flavour of fresh leaves used in Indian, Thai and other Eastern and Latin American cuisines. Now popular in salads and sauces. Crushed seeds much used in Greek and other Mediterranean dishes, such as ratatouille, terrines and pâtés.

Cumin *(Cuminum cyminum)*
Perfumed seeds, whole or ground, widely used in Middle-eastern, Indian and Latin American dishes, using beef, lamb, chicken and aubergines. Common in pickles and chutneys, as held to aid digestion.

Dill *(Anethum graveolens)*
Delicate flavour of fresh leaves works well with potatoes, cucumber and in salads and dressings. Also marries particularly well with fish and seafood and widely used in sauces and marinades.

Elder *(Sambucus nigra)*
Elderflowers impart their delicious flavour, akin to that of the muscat grape, to a wide variety of sweet dishes. As they cut acidity, especially popular with tart fruit, like rhubarb. Also used in jams and preserves and in making of wines and cordials.

Fennel *(Foeniculum vulgare)*
Delicate anise flavour of leaves is popular with fish, especially as a stuffing for oily fish. Crushed seeds used similarly. As also aids digestion of fat it is often used with fatty meat like pork.

Garlic *(Allium sativum)*
Related to the onion, this bulb is one of the world's most widely used flavourings. Popular crushed raw in sauces and dressings, it also features in a wide variety of cooked dishes. Garlic also has many valuable medicinal properties, including reducing blood clotting.

Geranium, scented *(Pelargonium)*
Leaves of different types have distinct delicate flavours: there are varieties with a rose scent, others with the flavours of oranges and apples. Used to flavour jellies, cakes and puddings, as well as summer drinks and cordials.

Horseradish *(Cochlearia armoracia)*
Hot and pungent taste of this root is traditional with roast beef. It also marries well with salmon, trout and mackerel and is good in fish pâtés. An aid to digestion, it is popular with fatty meats and fish.

Hyssop *(Hyssopus officinalis)*
Bitter leaves used sparingly in salads and in soups, stews and casseroles. Flowers are also used in salads.

Juniper *(Juniperus communis)*
Berries from this conifer are mild and resinous. Culinary application is limited, but they work well with game and in pâtés and are used in pickling.

Lavender *(Lavandula spica)*
Strongly scented flowers are crystallized for cake decoration or used to flavour jams and jellies.

Lemon balm *(Melissa officinalis)*
Delicate lemony leaves used in soups, salads, fish and poultry dishes and in custards, jellies and fruit compotes. Also popular in fruit and wine cups.

Lemon grass *(Cymbopogon citratus)*
This South-east Asian perennial has a strong lemon flavour and is popular in the cooking of the region. Dried and crushed it is known as *sereh* and has long been available in Asian shops. The fresh stalks are also now common in Western supermarkets.

Lemon verbena *(Aloysia triphylla)*
Highly perfumed leaves used sparingly to give lemon tang to poultry and fish dishes, milk puddings, fruit salads, sweet sauces and jams.

Lovage *(Levisticum officinale)*
Spicy celery flavour of leaves good with pulses and in soups, casseroles, cheese dishes and sauces. Earthy taste of seeds also used to flavour potato and rice dishes as well as breads and pastries.

Marigold *(Calendula officinalis)*
Fresh flower petals used for salads and as garnish. Dried they are used rather like saffron to give flavour and colour to cheese, rice and fish dishes, soups and stews, cakes and puddings.

Marjoram and oregano *(Origanum)*
Delicately sweet-scented leaves of Sweet marjoram *(O. majorana)* used fresh in salads and raw vegetable dishes and added to fish and meat dishes at the end of cooking. More robust French or Pot marjoram *(O. onites)* and Oregano *(O. vulgare)* dry well and are popular throughout the Mediterranean, especially on pizzas and in pasta sauces and Greek salads.

Mint *(Mentha)*
Family of refreshing leaves with delightfully different flavours. As well as familiar spearmint and peppermint, there are varieties which taste of apple, lemon, basil, eau de cologne, pineapple and ginger. Used widely in ice-creams and fruit dishes; also in savoury dishes, especially with lamb, peas and potatoes.

Nasturtium *(Tropaeolum majus)*
Leaves used to add distinctive peppery flavour to salads, sauces and sandwiches, while flowers are a common garnish. Seeds and buds used in pickles.

Parsley *(Petroselinum crispum)*
Probably most widely used culinary herb and base of bouquet garni. Best used raw or briefly cooked in soups, salads, sauces, fish and egg dishes. Flat-leaf variety has a stronger flavour than the curly-leaf.

Primrose *(Primula vulgaris)*
Fresh primrose flowers and young leaves are popular in salads and to flavour wine, jams and jellies and preserves, as well as some puddings and sorbets.

Purslane *(Portulaca oleracea)*
Young leaves used in salads and to flavour cheese and egg dishes and dips.

Rocket *(Eruca sativa)*
This member of the mustard family, very popular in Elizabethan cooking, is now enjoying a well-deserved revival in popularity as a salad addition.

Rosemary *(Rosmarinus officinalis)*
Pungently flavoured resinous leaves used sparingly in stews, roasts and marinades, especially in conjunction with lamb, pork and game. They may also be infused in milk for sweet puddings and used to flavour fruit desserts. Flowers are added fresh to salads or crystallized for a garnish.

Sage *(Salvia officinalis)*
Strongly aromatic leaves are used with pork, veal, game, liver and fatty meats. Also good with beans, pulses and cheeses. The many varieties have varying degrees of pungency, one even tasting of pineapple. The flowers are used in salads.

Salad burnet *(Poterium sanguisorba)*
Delicate flavour of leaf imparts nutty cooling cucumber flavour to salads and raw vegetable dishes. Also works well with soft cheeses, in creamy soups, egg dishes and in chilled mousses.

Savory, winter and summer *(Satureja montana and S. hortensis)*
Used like sage, summer savory leaves are traditionally teamed with pulses and beans, or used to flavour sausages, meat pies and soups. Winter savoury is combined with other herbs in sauces for game, duck and pork.

Sorrel *(Rumex scutatus/acetosa)*
Similar to spinach, leaves used sparingly in salads. Also good in egg dishes, sauces for fish and with potatoes, onions, tomatoes, lamb and beef.

Sweet cicely/myrrh *(Myrrhis odorata)*
Delicate sweet flavour of leaves and unripe seeds (fruit) has a hint of aniseed and is good in fruit tarts, pies and salads, ice-creams and sorbets. Particularly good with tart fruit like rhubarb and gooseberry. Leaves are also used in salads and omelettes.

Sweet violet *(Viola odorata)*
Delicately flavoured flowers added fresh to salads, used in fruit and wine cups, or infused to make syrup to flavour cakes, puddings and ice-creams. Flowers also crystallized for cake decorations.

Tarragon *(Artemisia dracunculus)*
One of the fines herbes, French tarragon has a wonderfully warm subtle flavour which goes particularly well with chicken, eggs and potatoes. It is also popular in salad dressings and sauces. Russian tarragon has coarser flavour.

Thyme *(Thymus)*
Essential ingredient in bouquet garni, has a strong flavour which develops on long slow cooking, especially with garlic, olive oil, tomatoes, onion and wine. Many different varieties with flavours which suit different uses; several are lemon-scented and work well with fish, seafood and chicken.

HERB COMBINATIONS
Bouquet garni
Basic constituents are a bunch of parsley stalks, 2 or 3 sprigs of thyme, and 1 or 2 bay leaves. They are commonly tied together with string or in a muslin sack so that they may easily be removed after cooking. Dried versions are available in sachets.

Bouquets garnis are used in almost all stocks, sauces, soups and stews. Apart from these basic constituents, there may also be additional ingredients, such as marjoram, fennel, tarragon, celery, savory, sage, garlic, leek, juniper, lemon and orange peel, according to the dish in which the bouquet garni is being used. Rosemary is always included in Provençal bouquets.

Fines herbes
Fresh chopped parsley, tarragon, chives and chervil, usually in equal quantities, form the most usual ingredients of this classic French flavouring. It is used in omelettes and other egg dishes, with soft cheeses and cooked vegetables and in herb butters.

Herbes de Provence
This combination traditionally consists of bay, thyme, rosemary, basil and savory. Most usually encountered dried, the mixture is particularly favoured for use with grilled meats and poultry.

SOUPS

Soups make a wonderful showplace for herbs. Whether in as simple a form as sprinkling chopped chives, parsley or coriander on a cream soup just before serving or by incorporating at an early stage of cooking the flavour of a strongly aromatic herb like lemon grass or horseradish, the addition of herbs can transform a soup entirely. Dried herbs used at the outset enliven an insipid stock or bland ingredients. Fresh herbs given the briefest of cooking or stirred in at the last minute bring sparkle to any soup. One or two handfuls of chopped mixed fresh herbs in a good stock make one of the tastiest and most refreshing of soups, without the need for any other additional ingredients save some sour cream to give it body. Serve this hot or chilled.

Left: Chilled Avocado Soup with Coriander (page 14); centre: Chilled Celeriac and Apple Soup with Chives (page 14)

CELERIAC *is a variety of celery grown for its large spherical fleshy white root. Long a favourite in France, it has recently become more widely available in this country. Usually boiled and puréed with potatoes, it is also popular shredded raw in salads or dressed with a RÉMOULADE sauce as a starter (see page 25).*

CHILLED AVOCADO SOUP WITH CORIANDER

2 ripe avocados
juice of ½ lemon
1 tsp chilli oil
3 tbsp finely chopped coriander
225 g/8 oz plain yogurt, preferably Greek
300 ml/½ pt crème fraîche
300 ml/½ pt fresh tomato juice
450 ml/¾ pt vegetable stock
½ onion, finely shredded
salt and freshly ground black pepper

Halve and stone the avocados. Peel them and place the flesh in a large bowl with the lemon juice. Mash with a fork or hand blender until smooth.

Stir in the chilli oil and two-thirds of the coriander. Cover and chill for 30 minutes.

Gently blend in the yogurt and crème fraîche, followed by the tomato juice and finally the stock. Stir in the shredded onion, season and chill for 2 hours.

Adjust the seasoning, if necessary, and garnish with the remaining coriander to serve.

CHILLED CELERIAC AND APPLE SOUP WITH CHIVES

55 g/2 oz butter
1½ large onions, sliced
½ tsp freshly grated nutmeg
3 hard green cooking apples, unpeeled and coarsely chopped
1 celeriac root, peeled and cut into small cubes
3 chicken stock cubes
2 tsp lime juice
bunch of chives
salt and freshly ground black pepper

Melt the butter in a large heavy-based pan over a moderate heat and sauté the onions in it for about 2-4 minutes, until translucent.

Sprinkle in the nutmeg and cook for another 1 minute. Add the apples and celeriac and cook for 5 minutes more, stirring constantly.

Dissolve the chicken stock cubes in 1.1 litre/2 pt of hot water and add this to the pan. Reduce the heat, cover and simmer for 30 minutes.

Remove the pan from the heat and allow it to cool a little before adding the lime juice. When cold, purée the soup in a blender or food processor. Then chill overnight.

Adjust the seasoning of the chilled soup and pour it into serving bowls. Finely snip the chives over the bowls to garnish.

HERBED CREAM OF CARROT SOUP

SERVES 4–6

450 g/1 lb carrots, chopped
450 ml/¾ pt vegetable stock
30 g/1 oz butter
1 large onion, diced
1 tsp celery salt
300 ml/½ pt single cream
½ tbsp each finely chopped watercress, parsley and chives
freshly ground black pepper

Put the carrots and the vegetable stock in a large pan and gently bring to the boil. Reduce the heat, cover and simmer for about 15 minutes, until the carrots are tender. Leave to cool in the pan.

Melt the butter in a frying pan over a moderate heat and sauté the onion until translucent. Add the celery salt and stir thoroughly. Remove from the heat and allow to cool.

Transfer the carrots and their stock to a blender or food processor. Add the onion and blend until smooth.

Return this to the saucepan and bring almost to the boil. Remove from the heat and add the cream. Season with pepper only and stir thoroughly over a gentle heat just to warm through. Do not allow to boil or the cream will curdle.

Pour the soup into warmed bowls and sprinkle a little of each of the 3 herbs over each bowl.

HERBED VEGETABLE SOUP WITH VERMICELLI

SERVES 6

1 tbsp butter or vegetable margarine
1 large onion, diced
2 crisp stalks of white celery, chopped
2 large carrots, chopped
2 heads of broccoli, chopped
1 large potato, diced
1 tbsp chopped oregano
1.5 litre/2½ pt vegetable stock
85 g/3 oz vermicelli
1 tbsp chopped flat-leaf parsley
1 tbsp chopped chives
salt and freshly ground black pepper

Melt the butter or margarine in a large heavy-based pan over a moderate heat and sauté the onion until translucent.

Add the other vegetables and sauté for 5 minutes, stirring constantly. Add the oregano and sauté for a further 2 minutes.

Add the stock and bring it gently to the boil. Cover and simmer gently for 10 minutes.

Add the vermicelli, increase the heat to moderate again and cook until the vermicelli is tender.

Adjust the seasoning, then add the parsley and chives just before serving.

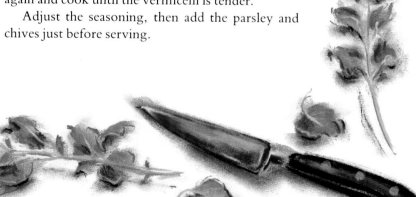

LEMON GRASS *is native to South-east Asia and its citrus tang is a basic flavour in much of the cooking of the area, especially Thai cuisine. It remains fibrous even after lengthy cooking so is best removed after it has imparted its flavour. Once available only from specialist food stores, or in its powdered form, known as* SEREH, *the long pale green stalks with bulbous bases are now a common sight in some supermarkets.*

ARTICHOKE SOUP WITH LEMON GRASS

SERVES 6

2 stalks of lemon grass
450 g/1 lb large Jerusalem artichokes, unpeeled and coarsely chopped
85 g/3 oz butter
2 large onions, sliced
1 garlic clove, finely chopped
1.1 litre/2 pt chicken stock
4 tbsp single cream (optional)
1 tbsp finely chopped parsley, to garnish

Bring a large pan of water to the boil.

Crush the bulb ends of the lemon grass stalks, then place them in the pan of water with the artichokes and simmer them for 10 minutes. Strain the artichokes, reserving the lemon grass.

Melt the butter in a large heavy-based pan over a moderate heat. Add the onions and garlic and sauté them for about 3 minutes. Reduce the heat, cover and simmer for a further 5 minutes.

Add the pieces of artichoke and stir them into the onions and garlic. Then add the stock and bring to the boil. Add the reserved lemon grass, cover and simmer for 20 minutes. Remove from heat and allow to cool. Remove and discard the lemon grass.

Liquidize the mixture in a blender or food processor. Return it to the pan and re-heat gently. Stir in the cream, if using, and adjust the seasoning.

Pour the soup into warmed serving bowls and garnish with parsley.

FISH CHOWDER WITH HORSERADISH

SERVES 6

450 g/1 lb skinned cod fillet
450 g/1 lb skinned smoked haddock fillet
1.1 litre/2 pt milk
450 g/1 lb potatoes, peeled and diced
575 ml/1 pt fish stock
55 g/2 oz butter
225 g/8 oz onions, sliced
1 tbsp finely grated fresh horseradish root
juice of ½ lemon
115 g/4 oz canned sweetcorn kernels (optional)
salt and freshly ground black pepper

Put the fish in a large pan and cover with the milk. Bring to just below the boil over a moderate heat and simmer gently for 20 minutes, or until the flesh flakes readily.

In another pan, put the potatoes and the fish stock. Bring to the boil and cook for 15 minutes.

Melt the butter in a frying pan over a moderate heat and sauté the onions for about 5 minutes, until translucent.

Pour the potatoes and their stock into the fish pan, then add the onions in their butter. Sprinkle the horseradish on top and mix gently. Add the lemon juice.

Slowly bring the contents of the pan to a simmer and cook very gently for 15 minutes. Season and add the sweetcorn, if using.

Pour into warmed bowls and serve immediately.

Clockwise from the left: Herbed Cream of Carrot Soup (page 15), Artichoke Soup with Lemon Grass and Fish Chowder with Horseradish

GREEN LENTIL SOUP WITH HERBES DE PROVENCE

225 g/8 oz green lentils, preferably Le Puy
30 g/1 oz butter
1 large onion, coarsely chopped
225 g/8 oz tomatoes, coarsely chopped
1 tbsp herbes de Provence
salt and freshly ground black pepper
1 tbsp chopped flat-leaf parsley, to garnish

Wash the lentils thoroughly, then put them in a large heavy-based pan with 850 ml/1½ pt of water. Bring to the boil, then simmer gently for 15-20 minutes

Chilled Raspberry and Mint Soup

until the lentils are tender. Set them aside in their stock.

Melt the butter in a frying pan over a moderate heat and add the onion. Sauté until translucent, then add the tomatoes and herbs and stir constantly for 5 minutes. Transfer the contents of the frying pan to the lentil pot. Season, cover and leave to cool.

When cool, purée the soup in a blender or food processor or push it through a sieve. Return to a moderate heat and gently warm it through.

Transfer the soup to warmed bowls and sprinkle with parsley to serve.

CHILLED RASPBERRY AND MINT SOUP*

juice of ½ lemon
675 g/1½ lb raspberries
1 tbsp demerara sugar
1 egg yolk
*(*see page 2 for advice on eggs)*
115 g/4 oz natural yogurt or fromage frais
1 tbsp finely chopped lemon mint
salt and freshly ground black pepper
4 mint sprigs, to garnish

Place all the ingredients in a blender or food processor, together with 300 ml/½ pt of water. Blend for 2 minutes. Strain the purée through a sieve.

Chill well for at least 2 hours. Season lightly and serve garnished with the whole mint sprigs.

CLEAR SEAFOOD SOUP WITH SAMPHIRE GRASS

1 tsp sugar
4 dried shiitake mushrooms
850 ml/1½ pt beef or chicken consommé
115 g/4 oz samphire grass
85 g/3 oz each small shelled mussels, shelled clams and peeled cooked prawns
freshly ground black pepper
2 tbsp finely chopped young leeks, to garnish
2 tbsp finely chopped chives, to garnish

Dissolve the sugar in a little warm water and soak the mushrooms in it for 30 minutes.

Remove them from the water and squeeze gently to remove excess liquid. Cut away any tough stalk and then slice the caps thinly.

Put the consommé in a large pan and add the sliced mushrooms and the samphire. Bring to the boil and simmer for 5 minutes.

Add the seafood, cover and simmer for a further 5 minutes. Season with freshly ground black pepper (salt should not be necessary due to the high mineral content of the samphire).

Ladle the soup into 4 warmed bowls, sprinkle with the chopped leeks and chives and serve immediately.

CHICKEN, LEMON AND RICE SOUP WITH BAY*

SERVES 6–8

30 g/1 oz butter
45 g/1½ oz flour
thinly pared rind and juice of 3 large unwaxed lemons
4 bay leaves
2 egg yolks
*(*see page 2 for advice on eggs)*
170 g/6 oz cooked chicken meat, coarsely chopped
115 g/4 oz cooked brown rice
salt and freshly ground black pepper

Melt the butter in a large heavy-based pan over a moderate heat. Stir in the flour and cook for 3 minutes, stirring constantly.

Slowly add 1.75 litre/3 pt of water, whisking constantly to avoid lumps. Add the lemon rind and bay leaves and simmer gently for 20 minutes.

In a large bowl, beat the egg yolks and slowly add the lemon juice, stirring constantly.

Remove the pan from the heat and slowly strain the liquid into the eggs, whisking gently. Return the mixture to the pan and bring to a very gentle simmer. Be careful not to allow the soup to boil at any stage or the egg will curdle.

Add the chicken and rice and season lightly. Allow to warm through very carefully for a minute or two and then serve in warmed bowls.

SHIITAKE MUSHROOMS *have been cultivated by the Japanese on oak bark for centuries. Dried shiitakes are now widely available in health-food shops. Some supermarkets even have them fresh.* SAMPHIRE GRASS, *prized for its salty iodine flavour, is available from better fishmongers.*

STARTERS AND SNACKS

S tarters should excite the palate to prepare it for what is to come. What better way to ensure this than to tease it with the intriguing complexity of the flavours of herbs? First courses also make fairly safe testing grounds to try more unusual flavour combinations. Moreover, some herbs are known to have properties which excite the digestive processes and encourage the assimilation of food: for instance the rosemary in *Gruyère, Rosemary and Tomato Toasties* helps the digestion of the cooked cheese. For those cooks preparing quick snacks and light meals in a hurry, the pungency of fresh herbs delivers a great deal of aroma and flavour without recourse to lengthy cooking processes.

Left: Gruyère, Rosemary and Tomato Toasties (page 22); right: Curried Eggs with Lemon Parsley Sauce (page 26)

PINEAPPLE MINT (Mentha rotundifolia) *has a very fruity tang. If it is difficult to find, try one of the many other varieties of mint with distinctive flavours:* applemint (M. sauveolens) *has a hint of apples;* eau de cologne *or* orange mint (M. piperita citrata) *has a very sharp bergamot-like scent and flavour;* ginger mint (M. gentilis) *is slightly spicy.*

If PURPLE BASIL (Ocimum basilicum 'Purpurascens') *is difficult to obtain, use the ordinary green variety, but the flavour will not be quite the same.*

GRUYÈRE, ROSEMARY AND TOMATO TOASTIES

MAKES 6

1 egg, lightly beaten
150 ml/¼ pt milk
3 slices of granary bread
55 g/2 oz butter
2 tsp Dijon mustard
85 g/3 oz Gruyère cheese, grated
3 tomatoes, sliced
large sprig of rosemary
salt and freshly ground black pepper

Mix the egg with the milk in a shallow dish and season well. Remove the crusts from the bread and cut each slice across diagonally into 2 triangles. Soak these in the egg mixture.

Melt the butter in a frying pan over a moderate heat and fry the egg-coated bread slices until golden on both sides. Remove and place on paper towels to drain off excess fat.

Preheat a moderate grill.

Spread the top of each toasty thinly with Dijon mustard then sprinkle with the cheese. Arrange the tomato slices on top and sprinkle spikes of rosemary over the tomato.

Place under the grill and cook until the cheese begins to bubble.

PINEAPPLE MINT AND CUCUMBER MOUSSE

SERVES 4–6

piece of cucumber, about 16 cm/6½ in long
285 g/10 oz cream cheese
2 tsp cider vinegar
1 tbsp finely chopped pineapple mint leaves
2½ tsp powdered gelatine
150 ml/¼ pt vegetable stock
salt and freshly ground black pepper
crispy lettuce leaves, to serve
6 sprigs of pineapple mint, to garnish
toast triangles, to serve

Cut 12-18 thin slices off the cucumber for garnish and reserve. Slice the rest thickly and put it in a blender or food processor with the cream cheese, vinegar and mint. Process until smooth and then season.

In a small pan, dissolve the gelatine in 2 tablespoons of the stock over a low heat. Allow to cool and then add this to the cheese mixture together with the remaining stock.

Blend once again until smooth. Adjust the seasoning, if necessary, and then place in a serving bowl. Cover and chill for at least 1 hour, until set firmly.

Set the bowl on a bed of crispy lettuce, garnish with mint sprigs and reserved cucumber slices and serve accompanied by toast triangles.

RICOTTA, OLIVE AND HERB RAMEKINS

SERVES 6

140 g/5 oz Ricotta cheese
140 g/5 oz fromage frais
75 g/2½ oz butter, softened
2 garlic cloves, crushed
1 tbsp each finely chopped deseeded red and green
sweet pepper
3 tbsp pine nuts
1½ tbsp each finely chopped stoned black and green olives
1 tbsp finely chopped purple basil leaves
1 tbsp finely chopped flat-leaf parsley
salt and freshly ground black pepper
½ cucumber, peeled and thinly sliced, to garnish
strips of purple basil leaves, to garnish

Line 6 ramekin dishes with film, leaving a large overhang all round to allow the dish to be covered.

Put the Ricotta, fromage frais, butter and garlic in a bowl and mix them thoroughly. Add the peppers, nuts, olives, basil and parsley and seasonings. Stir again to mix well.

Put the mixture in the lined moulds and smooth down the tops. Cover with the film overhangs and chill overnight.

Unwrap the top of the film from each ramekin, invert it to unmould it and remove the film. Garnish each with overlapping cucumber slices and basil strips to serve.

Top: Pineapple Mint and Cucumber Mousse; bottom: Ricotta, Olive and Herb Ramekins

Any blue cheese may be used in the recipe for HERBED BOUCHÉES WITH BLUE CHEESE CREAM, *but Roquefort gives the finest results. 'Bouchée' is the French for mouthful and has become associated with these little vol-au-vent pastries.*

CRUNCHY BEANS WITH LIME AND CORIANDER

450 g/1 lb fine green beans
30 g/1 oz butter
juice of 1 lime
1 tbsp finely chopped coriander
salt and freshly ground black pepper
slices of buttered sunflower seed bread, to serve

Bring a large pan of water to the boil, add some salt and the beans. Keeping the water boiling, cook the beans for only 3-5 minutes, depending on size, until just crunchy. Immediately drain, refresh under cold running water and drain again.

Melt the butter in a heavy-based pan over a moderate heat and add half the lime juice. Add the drained beans and toss them to coat them thoroughly in the butter and lime juice. Season, add half the coriander and toss again.

Empty the contents of the pan into a warmed serving bowl. Squeeze the remaining lime juice over and sprinkle with the remaining coriander. Serve immediately with the buttered sunflower seed bread.

HERBED BOUCHÉES WITH BLUE CHEESE CREAM

MAKES ABOUT 28

900 g/2 lb cold puff pastry
2 tsp herbes de Provence
2 eggs, beaten
115 g/4 oz blue cheese
55 g/2 oz cream cheese
1 tbsp finely chopped parsley

Preheat the oven to 220C/425F/gas7.

Roll out the pastry to a thick rectangle. Sprinkle the herbs uniformly over the pastry and roll them well in. The pastry should finish up about 6 mm/¼ in thick.

Using a 5 cm/2 in pastry cutter, cut out as many rounds of pastry as possible, re-rolling trimmings as necessary. Using a 2.5 cm/1 in pastry cutter, make a cut in the centre of each round about halfway through the pastry to make 'lids'.

Place the pastry rounds on a baking tray. Using a pastry brush, coat them lightly with the beaten egg. Bake in the oven for 10-12 minutes.

While still warm, use the tip of a sharp knife to prise off the 'lids' and reserve them.

In a bowl, mix the cheeses and the parsley together thoroughly. Using two teaspoons, fill the bouchées with this mixture.

Place the filled bouchées back in the oven for a few minutes to heat them through. Transfer to a warm serving dish, place the 'lids' back on and serve immediately.

ZAHTAR

SERVES 4–6

55 g/2 oz walnuts
55 g/2 oz hazelnuts
115 g/4 oz toasted sesame seeds
30 g/1 oz cumin seeds
55 g/2 oz coriander seeds
sprig of thyme
½ tsp fine salt
½ tsp crushed black peppercorns
4 tbsp extra virgin olive oil
6 chunky slices of brown bread, to serve

Using the slow pulse of a food processor, crush all the nuts and seeds with the thyme to a fine crumble - but be careful not to over-process. Transfer to a serving bowl, stirring in the salt and pepper.

Place the olive oil in another small serving bowl. Remove the crusts from all but one end of each slice of bread and cut each slice into 4–6 fingers.

To serve: dip the fingers of bread into the oil and then into the nut mixture.

CELERIAC RÉMOULADE WITH BERGAMOT

300 ml/½ pt ready-made mayonnaise
115 g/4 oz celeriac, finely shredded
1 onion, finely diced
1 tsp chopped capers
1 tsp chopped chervil
1 tsp chopped parsley
3 bergamot flowers
slices of crispbread, to serve

Put the mayonnaise in a bowl, add the celeriac and mix thoroughly. Add the onion and capers, then sprinkle in the herbs. Gently toss until well mixed.

Tear off the petals from one of the flowers and add these to the mixture. Cover with film and chill for 2 hours.

Uncover and serve garnished with the 2 remaining bergamot flowers. Serve with slices of crispbread.

STUFFED SNOW PEAS

SERVES 4–6

36 snow peas (see below)
55 g/2 oz crème fraîche
1 tbsp finely chopped dill
30 g/1 oz fromage frais
juice and grated zest of 1 unwaxed lime
55 g/2 oz mock caviar
salt and freshly ground black pepper
radicchio or lollo rosso leaves, to serve

Try to buy snow peas of a uniform size. Blanch them in boiling salted water for 2 minutes. Immediately drain, refresh under cold water, drain again and pat dry.

Using a sharp knife, slit the peas down one long side and open them carefully.

Put the crème fraîche in a bowl and mix in the dill and fromage frais. Add the lime juice and zest and seasonings, then gently fold in the mock caviar.

Use this mixture to stuff the cavities of the snow peas and serve immediately on a bed of colourful leaves.

ZAHTAR *is an aromatic mixture popular in many Arab nations. It is sprinkled on food as a condiment, spread on bread or used as a dip. In some places it is even sold by street traders in small paper bags.*

CURRIED EGGS WITH LEMON PARSLEY SAUCE*

SERVES 6

6 soft-boiled eggs, shelled and halved
½ tsp curry powder
2 tbsp double cream
½ tbsp finely chopped dill
1 large onion, finely chopped
55 g/2 oz mock caviar
salt and freshly ground black pepper
6 small parsley sprigs, to garnish
FOR THE LEMON AND PARSLEY SAUCE
2 egg yolks
*(*see page 2 for advice on eggs)*
115 g/4 oz unsalted butter
1 tbsp finely chopped parsley
juice of ½ lemon

Carefully remove the yolks from the hard-boiled egg halves and place the yolks in a bowl with the curry powder, cream, dill and onion. Mix thoroughly and season. Fill the cavities in the egg halves with the mixture.

Make the lemon and parsley sauce: put the egg yolks in a bowl set over a bain-marie or double boiler placed over a gentle heat and keep at a constant simmer.

Using a wooden spoon, beat the egg yolks for 2-3 minutes until the yolks begin to thicken. Add the butter, a few knobs at a time, beating constantly.

When all the butter has been incorporated, add the parsley and lemon juice. Season and remove from the heat, but keep warm.

Spoon the sauce into the middle of 6 plates. Using a circular movement, allow it to flood the entire surface of the inner part of the plate.

Place 2 egg halves in the middle of the pool of sauce on each plate, spoon the mock caviar over them and garnish with the parsley sprigs.

HERRING WITH FENNEL AND RED ONION

8 small herrings, heads removed
1 fennel bulb, thinly sliced
2 red onions, thinly sliced and separated into rings
2 cloves
4 bay leaves
8 allspice berries
8 green peppercorns
1 tsp salt
125 ml/4 fl oz tarragon vinegar
freshly ground black pepper
sprigs of fresh bay, to garnish

Remove the backbone from the fish by running the back of a spoon from the tail to the head while exerting firm pressure. It should then lift out quite cleanly.

Remove any stray bones and rinse the fish under cold running water. Pat dry, then lay flat on a clean surface with the flesh side uppermost.

Arrange the slices of fennel and the onion rings in the centre of the fish. Season and roll up the fish from the head to the tail and secure with cocktail sticks.

Place the rolled fish in a large heavy-based pan together with the cloves, bay leaves, allspice, green peppercorns, the teaspoon of salt and some pepper. Pour the vinegar over the fish, then add just enough water to cover the fillets.

Cover the pan, bring just to the boil and simmer very gently for 45-60 minutes, or until the flesh flakes easily when forked.

Carefully transfer the fillets to a deep serving dish and strain enough liquid over the fish to cover. Leave to cool completely then cover with film and chill overnight.

Remove the film and garnish the jellied fish with the sprigs of fresh bay. Serve immediately before the jelly begins to melt.

CEVICHE

2 whole fresh mackerel or 4 skinned mackerel fillets
5 tbsp lime juice
5 tbsp lemon juice
3 tbsp extra virgin olive oil
1 tbsp red wine vinegar
1 large onion, finely chopped
1 tsp chopped coriander
2 tbsp chopped flat-leaf parsley
1 fresh chilli pepper, deseeded and finely chopped
2 large tomatoes, peeled and chopped
1 ripe avocado
salt and freshly ground black pepper
tortilla chips, to serve

If using whole fresh fish, press out the backbone of each and remove. Cut the fish or the fillets into chunks about 1 cm/½ in across.

Place the pieces of fish in a shallow dish and pour over the lime and lemon juice. Season, cover and leave to marinate for 6 hours, turning once or twice.

Put the oil, vinegar, onion, coriander, parsley, chilli and tomatoes in another bowl and mix together thoroughly.

Drain the fish, reserving the juice. Mix the fish in with the herb and tomato mixture and transfer to a serving dish.

Halve and stone the avocado. Peel and slice the flesh thinly, then arrange the slices on top of the fish mixture. Using a pastry brush, coat the avocado with the reserved juice to prevent discoloration.

Season with salt and pepper and serve with tortilla chips.

Top: Smoked Trout and Dill in Halibut Cornets;
bottom: Ceviche

PEPPERED SMOKED MACKEREL PÂTÉ WITH HORSERADISH

4 peppered smoked mackerel fillets, skinned
30 g/1 oz butter, softened
150 ml/¼ pt single cream
3 tbsp coarsely chopped hazelnuts
1 tbsp lime juice
1 tbsp horseradish sauce
salt and freshly ground black pepper
slices of warm toast, to serve

Put all the ingredients into a blender or food processor with some seasoning. Process until smooth, then transfer to a serving bowl.

Serve with slices of warm toast.

SMOKED TROUT AND DILL IN HALIBUT CORNETS

170 g/6 oz smoked trout fillets, skinned and flaked
1 tbsp finely chopped dill
1 tbsp horseradish cream
350 g/12 oz very thin slices of smoked or fresh halibut
2 slices of brown toast
small bunch of chervil
juice of ½ lemon
juice of 1 lime
salt and freshly ground black pepper

Place the smoked trout, dill and horseradish in a small bowl. Season and mix together thoroughly.

Lay the halibut slices on a flat surface and cut them into 8 strips. Spread each piece with the smoked trout mixture, then roll up into a cornet.

Cut each slice of toast into 4 rectangles. Place on a serving dish, then sit the cornets on top of them.

Garnish with chervil. Dribble the fruit juice over and sprinkle with pepper just before serving.

CEVICHE *is a dish native to South America in which raw fish virtually 'cooks' in a lime juice marinade.*

Fresh and smoked HALIBUT *are available sliced like smoked salmon from better fishmongers and some supermarkets. Smoked eel or smoked salmon may be substituted.*

MAIN COURSES

When preparing main courses using herbs, all the classic time-honoured associations come to the fore . . . lamb with rosemary, fish with dill, chicken with tarragon and so on. However, slightly more adventurous combinations, like my *Sautéed Lamb Fillet with Fennel Sauce,* can be very rewarding. When preparing a roast, for example, if in doubt add the herb only at the last minute to a little of the gravy to make sure it is to your taste. If so, then next time spike the meat with the herb at an early stage or even marinate it. Herbs also have the power to transform fairly humble ingredients into impressive meals, for instance ordinary pork substituted in the recipe for *Wild Boar Cutlets with Apple and Juniper* may fool even the most sophisticated palate.

From left to right: Venison and Sage Patties with Pears (page 40), Roast Pheasant with Thyme Brandy Cream (page 39) and Wild Boar Cutlets with Apple and Juniper (page 39)

SEAFOOD IN HERB AND SAFFRON SAUCE

3 tbsp olive oil
1 onion, chopped
1 red sweet pepper, deseeded and sliced
1 green sweet pepper, deseeded and sliced
2 large garlic cloves, crushed
2 tsp paprika
115 g/4 oz prepared squid, coarsely chopped
4 tomatoes, peeled and coarsely chopped
½ tsp ground saffron
2 bay leaves
85 g/3 oz flaked almonds
175 ml/6 fl oz dry white wine
grated zest and juice of 1 unwaxed lime
300 ml/½ pt fish stock
115 g/4 oz peeled cooked prawns
115 g/4 oz shelled mussels
115 g/4 oz shelled scallops, halved if large
3 tbsp brandy
1 tbsp chopped dill
125 ml/4 fl oz single cream
salt and freshly ground black pepper
flat-leaf parsley, to garnish
hot crusty bread, to serve

Heat the oil in a large flameproof casserole over a moderate heat. Add the onion, peppers, garlic, paprika and squid and sauté gently for 10 minutes.

Stir in the tomatoes, saffron, bay leaves, almonds, wine, lime zest and juice and the stock. Bring to the boil and cook for 3 minutes. Season.

Reduce the heat and add the prawns, mussels and scallops. Mix thoroughly, cover and simmer for 5 minutes. Add the brandy and dill and simmer for 3 minutes more. Stir in the cream and adjust the seasoning, if necessary.

Garnish with parsley just before serving with hot crusty bread.

SAFFRON, *the dried stamens of a type of crocus, is one of the most ancient and valued of spices. As well as imparting a wonderful golden colour, it also gives a subtly strong flavour which works particularly well with fish and seafood, rice and some pastries.*

SWEDISH FISH SOUFFLÉ WITH DILL

SERVES 4–6

100 g/3½ oz butter, plus more for greasing
2 tbsp crisp breadcrumbs
4 eggs, separated
100 g/3½ oz flour
575 ml/1 pt milk
225 g/8 oz cooked smoked haddock, flaked
1 tbsp finely chopped dill
salt and freshly ground black pepper

Preheat the oven to 220C/425F/gas7 and grease an 18 cm/7 in ovenproof soufflé dish carefully with butter, making sure that the rim is also well coated. Then dust this layer of butter with the breadcrumbs, shaking out any excess.

Beat the egg whites to stiff peaks.

Melt the butter in a large heavy-based pan over a moderate heat. Stir in the flour and cook gently for 2 minutes. Slowly add the milk, stirring constantly. Reduce the heat and cook for a further 5 minutes.

Remove from the heat and add the egg yolks, one at a time, followed by the fish. Stir a spoonful of the egg whites into this mixture to loosen it and then carefully fold in the remaining egg whites together with the dill and seasoning to taste.

Fill the prepared dish with the soufflé mixture and tap the dish on a work surface to help the filling settle with a level top and no air pockets.

Stand the dish in another slightly larger dish and pour boiling water into this to about halfway up the sides of the inner soufflé dish.

Bake for 30–40 minutes, until the soufflé is well risen and golden brown. Serve immediately.

Left: Tuna Roulade with Dill and Capers (page 34); right: Seafood in Herb and Saffron Sauce

TUNA ROULADE WITH DILL AND CAPERS

SERVES 6-8

200 g/7 oz canned tuna in oil
4 eggs, separated
2 tbsp freshly grated Parmesan cheese
FOR THE FILLING
300 ml/½ pt milk
1 onion, quartered
2 large sprigs of parsley, finely chopped
1 bay leaf
30 g/1 oz butter
30 g/1 oz flour
4 hard-boiled eggs, shelled and coarsely chopped
1 tsp grated zest and 1 tsp juice from an unwaxed lemon
2 tbsp finely chopped dill leaves
1 tsp capers
salt and freshly ground black pepper

ROULADE *is the French term for rolled and stuffed items, especially used for meats and omelette mixtures, as with this* TUNA ROULADE. *Canned red salmon makes a good alternative to tuna.*

Preheat the oven to 200C/400F/gas6 and line a 33 x 23 cm/13 x 9 in Swiss roll tin with waxed paper.

Prepare the filling: pour the milk into a small pan and add the onion, parsley and bay leaf. Bring quickly to the boil. Cover and leave to infuse off the heat for at least 20 minutes.

Meanwhile, in a mixing bowl, mash the tuna with its oil to a purée using a hand blender or fork.

Beat the egg yolks lightly, then beat them into the mixture in the bowl. Season. Beat the egg whites to stiff peaks and gently fold them into the mixture.

Pour the mixture into the prepared tin and level with a spatula. Bake on the top shelf of the oven for 10-15 minutes, until well risen, firm and light golden in colour. Leave to cool in the tin.

Finish the filling: melt the butter in a saucepan over a moderate heat. Add the flour, stirring constantly for 2 minutes. Add the strained milk, stirring constantly, and gently bring to the boil. Reduce the heat and simmer for 3 minutes. Add the eggs, lemon zest and juice, the dill and the capers. Season.

Sprinkle a piece of waxed paper slightly larger then the Swiss roll tin with the Parmesan cheese. Turn the cooled roulade out on the paper and peel off the original waxed paper from the upturned base.

Re-heat the filling, if necessary, and spread the mixture over the roulade with a spatula, leaving a 2.5 cm/1 in margin all the way around.

By lifting one short end of the paper, roll up the roulade like a Swiss roll. Transfer to a serving dish, sprinkle any remaining Parmesan on the top and serve immediately, cut in thick slices.

GRILLED SALMON STEAKS WITH SAFFRON SAUCE

4 salmon steaks, each weighing about 170 g/6 oz
FOR THE MARINADE
2 tbsp lime juice
1 tbsp clear honey
5 tbsp hazelnut oil
salt and freshly ground black pepper
FOR THE SAFFRON SAUCE
¼ tsp ground saffron
150 ml/¼ pt dry white wine
2 egg yolks
300 ml/½ pt double cream
55 g/2 oz butter, cut into small chunks
1 tbsp lemon juice

Put the salmon steaks in a shallow dish. Mix together the marinade ingredients and season them well. Pour this over the fish, cover and leave to marinate in the refrigerator for 12 hours, turning from time to time.

Make the saffron sauce: dissolve the saffron in the wine in a small pan and heat gently, stirring constantly. Cover and simmer for 3 minutes. Remove from the heat and allow to cool.

In a bowl, mix the egg yolks with the cream. Stir in the cooled wine and saffron mixture. Return this mixture to the pan and heat gently, stirring constantly, until it thickens. Do not allow to boil. Remove from the heat but keep warm.

Preheat a hot grill. Drain the salmon steaks, pat them dry and grill them for about 4 minutes on each side.

While the steaks are cooking, strain the sauce through muslin. Then whisk in the butter, a little at a time, followed by the lemon juice and seasoning to taste.

Place the fish on a warmed serving dish, pour over the saffron sauce and serve immediately.

SAUTÉED LAMB FILLET WITH FENNEL SAUCE

SERVES 6

2 tbsp walnut oil
900 g/2 lb lamb fillet, cut into 1 cm/½ in slices
¼ tsp salt
freshly ground black pepper
FOR THE FENNEL SAUCE
150 ml/¼ pt vegetable stock
2 fennel bulbs, thinly sliced, with the feathery leaves reserved for garnish
30 g/1 oz butter
1 tbsp flour
300 ml/½ pt single cream
salt and freshly ground black pepper

First make the sauce: put the stock in a pan with the fennel. Cover, bring to the boil and then cook over a moderate heat for 25 minutes. Remove from the heat and allow to cool.

When cool, liquidize the mixture in a blender or food processor and then push through a fine sieve.

Melt the butter in a pan over a moderate heat, add the flour and cook, stirring constantly, for 3 minutes.

Remove from the heat and stir in the sieved fennel purée. Return to the heat and stir constantly for 5 minutes. Gradually add the cream and then season to taste.

Heat the walnut oil in a frying pan over a moderate heat and add the lamb fillet slices. Sprinkle with the salt and some pepper, increase the heat and sauté the fillet, stirring constantly, for 3 minutes.

Transfer the lamb to a warmed serving dish, cover with the fennel sauce and garnish with the reserved fennel fronds to serve.

NUT OILS, *such as those made by pressing walnuts and hazelnuts, have fine strong nutty flavours. Excellent in moderation in salad dressings, they are available from good food stores and better supermarkets. Buy them in small quantities as a little goes a long way and they do go rancid quickly.*

HERBED LEG OF LAMB WITH TOMATO SAUCE

SERVES 6–8

boned leg of lamb, weighing about 1.35 k/3 lb
3 small sprigs of rosemary
½ tsp each snipped basil, thyme and oregano
rock salt and freshly ground black pepper
FOR THE SAUCE
1 tsp olive oil
2 onions, coarsely chopped
2 garlic cloves, crushed
1 green sweet pepper, deseeded and thinly sliced
1 red sweet pepper, deseeded and thinly sliced
400 g/14 oz canned peeled tomatoes, drained
1 tbsp tomato paste
115 g/4 oz oyster mushrooms, coarsely chopped
150 ml/¼ pt dry white wine

Preheat the oven to 230C/450F/gas8.

Lay the meat out flat and sprinkle it with the herbs, rock salt and freshly ground black pepper. Roll up as tightly as possible, then tie with string.

Place in a roasting pan and roast for 25 minutes. Reduce the temperature to 220C/425F/gas7 and cook for a further 45-50 minutes. Transfer to a warmed serving plate and keep warm.

Make the sauce: put the olive oil in a heavy-based pan over a moderate heat, then add the onions and garlic and sauté for 3-5 minutes, until translucent.

Add the peppers and combine thoroughly with the onions. Cook for 2 minutes, then add the tomatoes, tomato paste and the mushrooms. Stir well and cook for 2 minutes.

Season and add the wine. Increase the heat and bring to the boil, stirring constantly. Continue to boil to reduce a little, then serve with the lamb.

Left: Herbed Leg of Lamb with Tomato Sauce; Broccoli and Cauliflower with Five-herb Butter (page 45)

CHICKEN BAKED WITH SAVORY AND ORANGE

1 tbsp freshly grated peeled root ginger
½ tsp ground cloves
¾ level tbsp flaked rock salt
1 tsp coarsely ground black pepper
½ tsp ground coriander seeds
8 sprigs of winter savory
45 g/1½ oz butter, softened
1 large fresh oven-ready chicken, cut into quarters
1½ tbsp juice and the thinly pared rind from 1 unwaxed orange, cut into julienne strips
170 g/6 oz dry white wine

Preheat the oven to 200C/400F/gas6.

Place the ginger, cloves, salt, black pepper, coriander seeds and 2 sprigs of winter savory in a blender or food processor and pulse gently until reduced to a fine powder. In a bowl, blend this mixture into the softened butter.

Lift the skin gently from the chicken quarters and make several incisions into the flesh. Fill the incisions with the butter mixture, then cover over with the skin, securing with cocktail sticks.

Line a baking dish with foil and place the remaining winter savory sprigs on the base of the pan. Put the chicken on top of the savory, then pour over the orange juice.

Cook in the oven for 40-50 minutes, until tender and the juices run clear when a skewer is inserted in the thickest part of the thigh. Transfer the chicken to a warmed serving dish and keep warm.

Place the orange rind strips in the base of a small pan and add the wine. Cover and simmer gently for 3 minutes. Add the pan juices and the savory from the pan and bring to the boil. Boil rapidly for 2 minutes to reduce slightly.

Strain the sauce into a warmed jug and serve with the chicken.

A wide variety of herbs will work in the HERBED LEG OF LAMB. The traditional mint or parsley go especially well.

CHICKEN BREASTS WITH COCONUT TARRAGON CREAM

45 g/1½ oz butter
1 tbsp hazelnut oil
2 tbsp chopped tarragon
4 large fresh skinned chicken breast
2 tbsp coconut cream
salt and freshly ground black peppe

Melt the butter with the oil in a heavy based pan over a moderate heat. Add half the tarragon, followed by the chicken breasts. Cover and cook for about 5 minutes.

Remove the lid and turn the chicken breasts over. Season, increase the heat a little and cook for a further 5 minutes.

Reduce the heat to moderate and add the coconut cream. Baste the chicken and adjust the seasoning, if necessary.

Increase the heat again, turn the breasts once more and cook for a further 2 minutes.

Transfer the chicken and its sauce to a warmed serving dish and garnish with the remaining tarragon.

Note: this dish works equally well with more economical pieces of chicken such as drumsticks, thighs or wings.

Left: Falafel (page 41); right: Chicken Breasts with Coconut Tarragon Cream

ROAST PHEASANT WITH THYME BRANDY CREAM

SERVES 4–6

2 large oven-ready pheasants
2 unwaxed oranges, quartered
2 unwaxed lemons, quartered
75 g/2½ oz butter
55 g/2 oz slices of streaky bacon
1 tbsp hazelnut oil
4 onions, chopped
4 bay leaves
2 large sprigs of thyme
2 tbsp brandy
300 ml/½ pt double cream
salt and freshly ground black pepper
large bunch of watercress, to garnish

Preheat the oven to 230C/450F/gas8.

Wipe the pheasants thoroughly inside and out and stuff the cavities with alternating orange and lemon quarters.

Place the birds in a roasting pan and smooth 30 g/ 1 oz of the butter over each pheasant, using a spatula. Cover the breasts with the bacon. Season and pour 150 ml/¼ pt of water into the pan.

Place on the middle shelf of the oven and cook for 45 minutes, basting frequently with the pan juices.

Towards the end of this time, melt the remaining butter with the hazelnut oil in a saucepan over a moderate heat. Add the onions and sauté gently until translucent. Add the bay leaves and sprinkle the thyme into the onions. Cover and simmer for 5 minutes.

When the pheasants are cooked, use a spoon to squash the oranges and lemons into the birds' cavities, then tip the juice into the pan. Remove and discard the citrus quarters, place the pheasants on a warmed serving platter and keep hot.

Add the roasting pan juices to the onion mixture

and increase the heat. Warm the brandy in a small pan over a very low heat and add it to the sauce. Then gently stir in the cream, taking care that it does not boil. Adjust the seasoning, if necessary, and transfer to a warmed jug.

Serve the carved birds garnished with the watercress and the pieces of roast bacon bard, and accompanied by the sauce.

WILD BOAR CUTLETS WITH APPLE AND JUNIPER

8 wild boar cutlets or large pork chops
575 ml/1 pt buttermilk
8 juniper berries, crushed
6 crab apples or red Cox's, unpeeled, cored and sliced
½ tbsp cornflour
salt and freshly ground black pepper

In a shallow pan, marinate the cutlets or chops in the buttermilk for 36 hours.

Preheat a hot grill.

Remove the cutlets or chops and reserve the buttermilk. Pat the meat dry. Season the juniper berries with salt and pepper and press this mixture on both sides of the pieces of meat. Grill for 5-10 minutes on each side, until cooked as desired.

While the cutlets or chops are cooking, put the buttermilk in a heavy-based pan and add the apple slices. Bring to the boil and then simmer gently for 5 minutes.

In a small bowl, add 2 tablespoons of the buttermilk to the cornflour and mix thoroughly. Add this back to the buttermilk and apple mixture and bring to the boil, stirring continuously. Reduce the heat and simmer gently for 3 minutes, still stirring. Season.

Serve the sauce immediately to accompany the cooked cutlets or chops.

Although increasingly rare, WILD BOAR is still found in many parts of Europe. It is available in this country occasionally from better butchers. The dark red meat is low in fat and has a rich gamy flavour. Something approaching this may be reproduced using well-aged pork in a juniper berry marinade or sauce.

RABBIT CASSEROLE WITH MUSTARD AND MARJORAM

SERVES 6

125 ml/4 fl oz vegetable oil
1 oven-ready rabbit, weighing about 1-1.35 k/2¼-3 lb,
cut into pieces
2 tbsp Dijon mustard
4 tbsp flour
2 tbsp tomato paste
3 bay leaves
1 tsp dried marjoram
300 ml/½ pt vegetable stock
300 ml/½ pt red wine
2 garlic cloves, crushed
1 tsp salt
225 g/8 oz slices of back bacon, rinds removed
freshly ground black pepper
4 slices of brown bread, to garnish

Preheat the oven to 180C/350F/gas4.

Heat half the oil in a deep sauté pan over a moderate heat and brown the pieces of rabbit on all sides.

Using a slotted spoon, transfer the browned rabbit pieces to a large ovenproof casserole. Using a spatula, spread them with the Dijon mustard.

Add the flour and tomato paste to the oil in the sauté pan and cook for 2 minutes, stirring constantly. Add the herbs, stock and wine, followed by the garlic. Season with the 1 teaspoon of salt and some pepper. Bring to the boil and cook for a further 2 minutes.

Pour the sauce over the rabbit, cover the casserole and cook in the oven for 2½ hours.

Roll the bacon rashers up, then halve these rolls. Skewer them with cocktail sticks and dry-fry them until well browned. Add them to the casserole 30 minutes before the end of cooking time.

About 10 minutes before the end of cooking time, cut each slice of bread into 4 triangles. Heat the remaining oil in a frying pan until very hot and then fry the bread triangles until golden brown.

Adjust the seasoning of the casserole, if necessary and serve garnished with the bread croûtes.

VENISON AND SAGE PATTIES WITH PEARS

SERVES 6

675 g/1½ lb minced venison
1 tbsp grated zest and 3 tbsp juice from an unwaxed lemon
½ tbsp finely chopped sage
1 bay leaf, crushed
½ tbsp chopped parsley
12 slices of streaky bacon, rinds removed
6 fresh pears, peeled, sliced and warmed
salt and freshly ground black pepper

Mix the venison, lemon zest and juice, sage, bay leaf and parsley in a bowl. Cover and leave to marinate for 24 hours.

Preheat a hot grill.

Season the marinated mixture and form it into 6 patties. Wrap 2 slices of bacon around each one and secure with wooden cocktail sticks. Grill for 6 minutes on each side.

Place on a warmed serving dish and arrange the warmed pear slices decoratively on top to serve.

COURGETTE, TOMATO AND GARLIC FLAN

170 g/6 oz shortcrust pastry
350 g/12 oz courgettes
2 eggs, beaten
150 ml/¼ pt milk
150 ml/¼ pt double cream
2 garlic cloves, crushed
1 tsp tomato paste
1 tsp Worcestershire sauce
¼ tsp freshly grated nutmeg
115 g/4 oz tomatoes, sliced
salt and freshly ground black pepper
butter or margarine, for greasing

Preheat the oven to 200C/400F/gas6 and grease an 18 cm/7 in flan tin with some butter or margarine.

Roll out the pastry and use it to line the flan tin. Line with greaseproof paper and weight with some dried beans. Bake blind for 15 minutes. Leave to cool and then remove beans and lining paper.

Grate the courgettes and then blanch the shreds for 30 seconds only in boiling salted water. Drain, refresh under cold running water and set aside.

In a bowl, thoroughly mix the eggs, milk, cream, garlic, tomato paste, Worcestershire sauce, nutmeg and seasonings. Add the well-drained courgettes and then spread this mixture evenly in the pastry case. Arrange the tomatoes decoratively on the top.

Bake for 30-40 minutes, until the filling is set and golden in colour.

FALAFEL

MAKES 14–16

400 g/14 oz firm cooked chickpeas
2 onions, finely chopped
½ tsp turmeric
½ tsp cayenne pepper
1 tsp ground coriander
1 tsp ground cumin
2 garlic cloves, crushed
1 tbsp wholemeal flour
2 tbsp brown breadcrumbs
½ tsp baking powder
salt and freshly ground black pepper
vegetable oil, for deep-frying
more wholemeal flour, for dusting (optional)

Place the chickpeas, onions, spices, garlic, flour, breadcrumbs and baking powder in a blender or food processor and pulse gently until thoroughly mixed. Cover and leave to rest for 45 minutes.

Shape the mixture into balls (if too sticky, roll lightly in wholemeal flour).

Put the oil in a deep pan and heat to 195C/385F (a small cube of dry bread browns in 20 seconds). Deep-fry the balls, a few at a time, removing and draining each batch on paper towels when they are golden brown. Keep warm on a warmed serving dish until all are cooked.

Serve accompanied by a tomato salad.

FALAFEL *are rissoles made from spiced purées of beans or chickpeas. Egyptian in origin, they are now popular throughout the Middle East. Being high in proteins, they are a favourite dish with vegetarians.*

VEGETABLES AND SALADS

*I*t is in the preparation of vegetables and salads that most fresh herbs really come into their own. As well as marrying their flavours wonderfully well with those of the other ingredients, many have the power to bring out the basic flavour of the other vegetables and leaves. Moreover, a simple herb butter, mayonnaise or sauce can transform a plainly boiled or steamed vegetable from a humdrum accompaniment into a glorious feast in its own right. In salads, fresh herbs can be enjoyed for their texture as well as their taste. Salads are also the perfect place to use herb flowers, for both their interesting flavours and their very decorative appearance. Pour dressing over flowers only at the very last minute, if at all, or they will discolour.

Left: Baked Beetroot with Horseradish Cream (page 44); right: Green and White Bean Salad with Mint (page 44)

BAKED BEETROOT WITH HORSERADISH CREAM

4 large beetroots
1 tbsp horseradish cream
2 tbsp single cream
salt and freshly ground black pepper

BAKED
BEETROOT WITH
HORSERADISH
CREAM *makes an*
excellent first course.

The FIVE-HERB
BUTTER *works*
equally well with
most vegetables,
especially new
potatoes and leeks,
and is delicious with
steaks and fish.

Preheat the oven to 200C/400F/gas6.

Wash the beetroots gently, trying not to bruise their outer skin. Leave the root and stalk intact if possible. Place them in a foil-lined baking pan and cook in the oven for 50-60 minutes, until soft all the way through.

Gently lift the beetroots from the oven pan, cut off the root ends and halve the beetroots. Place the 2 halves of each beetroot cut side up on each of 4 warmed plates.

Mix the horseradish and cream. Season and serve cold with the hot beetroot. Alternatively, warm the mixture in a double-boiler and serve hot with the beetroot.

GREEN AND WHITE BEAN SALAD WITH MINT

225 g/8 oz flageolet beans, soaked overnight
225 g/8 oz haricot beans, soaked overnight
1 large courgette, thinly sliced
1 large onion, thinly sliced
1 large green sweet pepper, deseeded and coarsely chopped
1 large red sweet pepper, deseeded and coarsely chopped
2 large tomatoes, deseeded and coarsely chopped
4 garlic cloves, crushed
1 tbsp coarsely snipped fresh mint
1 tbsp finely chopped fresh parsley
grated zest of 1 unwaxed lemon
100 ml/3½ fl oz extra virgin olive oil
2 tbsp white wine vinegar
salt and freshly ground black pepper

Drain the beans, cover them with fresh cold water and bring it to the boil. Drain and repeat the process. When boiling for the second time, cover, reduce the heat and simmer for about 60 minutes, until the beans are tender. Top up the water level from time to time, as necessary.

Drain the beans and refresh them under cold running water. When thoroughly drained, place them in a salad bowl.

Add the other ingredients except the oil and vinegar. Toss gently to mix well.

Mix the oil and vinegar and season to taste. Pour this over the salad and toss again before serving.

BROCCOLI AND CAULIFLOWER WITH FIVE-HERB BUTTER

SERVES 4–6

225 g/8 oz broccoli florets
225 g/8 oz cauliflower florets
salt

FOR THE HERB BUTTER
115 g/4 oz butter
½ tsp each finely chopped marjoram, mint, chives and tarragon
1 tsp finely chopped parsley
1 tbsp lemon juice

Several hours before, make the herb butter: cream the butter in a bowl until light. Gently work in the herbs and lemon juice. Leave at room temperature for 2 hours to allow the herbs to release their flavours and then chill for 1-2 hours.

Blanch the broccoli and cauliflower florets in boiling salted water for 3-5 minutes, depending on the desired degree of crunchiness.

Using a wire skimmer or slotted spoon, transfer the vegetables to a colander and refresh under cold water. Then return the florets to the boiling water for 1 minute only to re-heat.

Transfer to a warmed serving dish, dot with knobs of the herb butter and serve immediately.

HUNGARIAN MARROW

1 young marrow
75 g/2½ oz butter
1 onion
½ tsp caraway seeds
3 tbsp white wine vinegar
2 tsp paprika
½ tsp caster sugar
115 g/4 oz single cream
1 tsp finely chopped dill
salt and freshly ground black pepper

For a spicier version of HUNGARIAN MARROW, *try using cayenne to taste instead of paprika.*

Peel the marrow and cut it into quarters. Scoop out and discard the seeds. Slice the flesh thinly.

Melt the butter in a large pan over a high heat, add the marrow slices and cook quickly for 5 minutes, turning constantly. Remove the marrow from the pan and keep warm.

Place the onion and caraway seeds in the pan and cook for 2 minutes. Add the vinegar and paprika and cook for a further 5 minutes over a moderate heat. Add the sugar and stir until it is completely dissolved.

Reduce the heat, then add the cream followed by the marrow and the dill, stirring to coat evenly. Cover and simmer very gently for 3 minutes, taking care that the contents of the pan do not boil.

Adjust the seasoning and serve in a warmed dish.

TOMATO, THYME AND SPINACH TARTLETS

55 g/2 oz butter, plus more for greasing
675 g/1½ lb wholemeal shortcrust pastry
2 onions, thinly sliced
1 tsp dried thyme
115 g/4 oz freshly grated Parmesan cheese
55 g/2 oz puréed cooked spinach
1 tbsp Dijon mustard
4 eggs, beaten
115 g/4 oz crème fraîche
6 small tomatoes, thinly sliced
salt and freshly ground black pepper

Preheat the oven to 180C/350F/gas4 and grease 18 small tartlet trays with butter.

On a cold surface, roll out the pastry to a thickness of about 3 mm/⅛ in. Use to line the prepared trays, re-rolling the trimmings, if necessary. Cover and chill.

Melt the butter in a pan over a low heat, add the onions and sauté until translucent, adding the thyme halfway through. Cook for about 6 minutes. Remove from the heat and allow to cool.

Spoon this mixture into the base of the tartlets, then sprinkle with half the Parmesan. Do not over-fill.

In a bowl, combine the remaining ingredients, except the tomatoes. Season the mixture and pour it into the tartlet cases.

Arrange the tomato slices on the top, sprinkle over the remaining Parmesan and bake for 15-20 minutes, until the filling is set and golden.

Left: Tomato, Thyme and Spinach Tartlets; right: Crispy Bacon, Bean and Parsley Salad (page 51)

TOMATO, THYME
AND SPINACH
TARTLETS *make*
excellent
accompaniments to
any pulse dish.
Made in four larger
tartlet pans, they
may also be served as
starters, snacks or
picnic food.

VEGETARIAN BAKE WITH SAGE HOLLANDAISE*

SERVES 6

3 tbsp hazelnut oil, plus more for greasing
2 onions, coarsely chopped
3 beef tomatoes, coarsely chopped
115 g/4 oz oyster mushrooms, coarsely chopped
1 tsp herbes de Provence
1 tbsp light soy sauce
85 g/3 oz buckwheat
30 g/1 oz brown rice
1 egg, beaten
150 ml/¼ pt vegetable stock
1 tbsp crushed hazelnuts
freshly ground black pepper
2 large sage leaves, for garnish
FOR THE GOLDEN SAGE HOLLANDAISE SAUCE
1 tbsp finely snipped golden sage
2 tbsp lemon juice
1 tbsp white wine vinegar
200 g/7 oz unsalted butter
1 tbsp dry white wine
3 egg yolks
*(*see page 2 for advice on eggs)*
salt and freshly ground black pepper

The SAGE HOLLANDAISE sauce also goes very well with chicken and veal and with rice, cheese and tomato dishes.

Preheat the oven to 190C/375F/gas5 and lightly grease an 18 cm/7 in shallow loaf tin with a little hazelnut oil.

Heat the hazelnut oil in a pan over a moderate heat. Add the onions, tomatoes and mushrooms, toss gently to coat evenly and cook for 3 minutes. Add the herbs and the soy sauce and cook for a further 2 minutes. Add the buckwheat and rice and cook for 2 minutes more. Then stir in the egg.

Add the vegetable stock and bring to the boil, stirring constantly. Reduce the heat, cover and simmer for 20–25 minutes, or until all the liquid has been absorbed. Season and add the hazelnuts.

Transfer the mixture to the prepared tin and bake for 45 minutes.

While it is baking, make the hollandaise sauce: mix the chopped sage with 1 tablespoon of the lemon juice, the vinegar and 1 tablespoon of water in a small pan and bring them to the boil. Strain off and discard the liquid, reserving the sage. Melt 170 g/6 oz of the butter in a heavy-bottomed pan over a gentle heat. Transfer to a warmed jug.

Place the egg yolks in the same pan and beat them quickly with a whisk. Add half the remaining lemon juice and all the wine together with a pinch of salt. Beat again. Add half the remaining unmelted butter and place the pan in a bain-marie or double boiler.

Whisking steadily, cook gently until the egg yolks are creamy and beginning to thicken. Immediately remove the pan from the heat and stir in the remaining unmelted butter until it dissolves.

Dribble the melted butter into the yolk mixture whisking fast. Add the butter more rapidly as the sauce thickens. When the sauce is the consistency of double cream, add the remaining lemon juice with the reserved sage and adjust the seasoning.

Serve the sauce with the hot vegetarian bake, garnished with the whole sage leaves.

VINE LEAVES STUFFED WITH CORIANDER RICE

225 g/8 oz preserved vine leaves or 40 fresh leaves
400 g/14 oz cooked brown rice
2 tbsp tomato paste
2 onions, diced
2 garlic cloves, crushed
1 tsp ground cinnamon
2 tbsp finely chopped coriander
1 tbsp currants
1 tbsp flaked almonds
2 tbsp walnut oil
juice of 2 limes
450 ml/¾ pt vegetable stock
salt and freshly ground black pepper

Place the fresh vine leaves in a large bowl and scald them thoroughly with boiling water. If using preserved leaves, allow them to soak for 10 minutes.

Drain the leaves, refresh under cold water and separate out on paper towels, dull side up.

In a bowl, combine the rice, tomato paste, onions, garlic, cinnamon, coriander, currants, almonds and salt and pepper.

Place 10 leaves in the base of a flameproof casserole. Cut any stems from the other leaves and place a scant tablespoon of the filling in the centre of each leaf. Fold the stem end of each leaf over the filling, then fold in the sides and continue to roll up the leaf carefully from the stem end to form a firm package about 5 cm/2 in long.

Place these side by side, seam side down, in the casserole. Sprinkle with the walnut oil and lime juice, and add just enough vegetable stock to cover them. If necessary, add a little water.

Cover the casserole and bring it to a gentle simmer. Simmer over a low heat for 1 hour. Throughout this time check that the vine leaves remain moist.

Transfer to a warmed serving dish and serve any excess liquid as a sauce.

If serving cold, leave to cool in the covered casserole dish, then transfer to a serving dish.

If VINE LEAVES are difficult to obtain, use large spinach or Swiss chard leaves. The rice stuffing may also be flavoured with minced lamb or chicken.

WATERCRESS, MANDARIN AND PRIMROSE SALAD

2 bunches of watercress
115 g/4 oz lamb's lettuce
115 g/4 oz canned mandarins in juice, drained
½ unwaxed orange
¾ tbsp Dijon mustard
3 tbsp oil
2 tbsp white wine vinegar
1 tbsp fresh orange juice
1 tsp finely chopped fresh tarragon
2 tsp finely chopped primrose leaves
salt and freshly ground black pepper
4 primrose flower heads, to garnish (optional)

Mix the watercress and lamb's lettuce in a salad bowl. Arrange the mandarin segments over the salad.

Peel the orange, discarding as much pith as possible. Slice the flesh thinly and cut the rind into fine julienne strips. Add these to the salad.

Combine the mustard, oil, vinegar, orange juice and tarragon in a screw-top jar. Shake vigorously, then season.

Shake the jar again well before dressing the salad. Arrange the chopped primrose leaves on the salad and serve.

Toss again at the table and garnish with the whole primrose flower heads, if using.

Left: Vegetarian Bake with Sage Hollandaise (page 48); right:
Watercress, Mandarin and Primrose Salad

CRISPY BACON, BEAN AND PARSLEY SALAD

675 g/1½ lb canned broad beans, drained
6 slices of streaky bacon, rinds removed
10 dried apricots, sliced into thin slivers
3 tbsp coarsely chopped hazelnuts
1½ tbsp coarsely chopped parsley
6 tbsp olive oil
2 tbsp wine vinegar
1 scant tbsp coarse-grain mustard
salt and freshly ground black pepper

Rinse the beans under cold running water, drain and dry on paper towels.

Dry-fry the bacon over a moderate to high heat until crispy. Cut the cooked bacon coarsely into pieces with scissors. Drain the pieces on paper towels to remove excess fat.

Place the beans in a salad bowl. Add the bacon, apricots, hazelnuts and parsley and toss well.

Pour the oil and vinegar into a screw-top jar. Add the mustard, seal and shake vigorously. Season with salt and pepper and shake again. Pour over the salad and toss well to serve.

The flowers and leaves of all varieties of Primrose *are edible.*

COURGETTE AND PURPLE BASIL SALAD

SERVES 4–6

675 g/1½ lb courgettes, coarsely grated
3 tomatoes, coarsely chopped
2 onions, thinly sliced
1 tbsp blue poppy seeds
2 tbsp extra virgin olive oil
1 level tbsp finely snipped purple basil leaves
1 tbsp tamari sauce
1 tbsp Japanese rice vinegar
freshly ground black pepper

Put the courgettes, tomatoes, onions and poppy seeds in a salad bowl and gently mix.

Put the oil, basil, tamari, rice vinegar and pepper in a screw-top jar and shake vigorously. Dress the salad with the mixture, toss well and serve.

TAMARI SAUCE *is a fine Japanese soy sauce made by fermentation. If unobtainable, use a good light soy sauce. If* JAPANESE RICE VINEGAR *is difficult to obtain, use light cider vinegar.*

TAHINI PASTE, *made from crushed sesame seeds, is a common Middle-eastern condiment. It is available from delicatessens and supermarkets.*

CHICKEN SALAD WITH SESAME CUCUMBER SAUCE

6 chicken fillets, skinned
1 tbsp freshly grated peeled root ginger
4 spring onions, including the green tops
2 small cucumbers
1 Iceberg lettuce, to serve
FOR THE SESAME CUCUMBER SAUCE
1 tsp peanut oil
1 tsp chilli oil
¼ tsp dry mustard
1 tbsp light soy sauce
2 tbsp tahini paste
1 tbsp rice vinegar
2 tbsp water
½ tsp salt
1 tbsp finely chopped green spring onion tops
1 tbsp roasted sesame seeds
salt and freshly ground black pepper

Place the chicken fillets in a pan with the ginger, spring onions and 700 ml/1¼ pt of water and bring to the boil. Cover and simmer gently for 4 minutes. Remove from the heat, but leave the chicken to cool in the stock.

Peel the cucumbers, reserving some of the skin. Halve them, scoop out the seeds and place the halves on beds of the lettuce arranged on 4 plates.

Using scissors, cut the drained chicken fillets into thin slivers and arrange these in the cucumber. If preparing in advance, cover with film and chill.

Make the sauce: combine all the ingredients except the spring onions and sesame seeds in a blender or food processor. Season, then add the onions and sesame seeds and toss together. Spoon this over the chicken.

Serve garnished with the reserved cucumber peel cut into thin slivers.

PARMA HAM AND FRESH FIG SALAD WITH MINT AND LIME CREAM DRESSING

SERVES 6

6 slices of Parma ham
10 mint leaves
juice of 2 limes
18 fresh figs
150 ml/¼ pt crème fraîche
170 g/6 oz radicchio or lollo rosso
salt and freshly ground black pepper
sprigs of mint, to garnish

Cut the ham into strips and cover with film to stop it drying out.

Using a pestle and mortar, bruise and crush the mint leaves in the lime juice and leave the mixture to infuse at room temperature for about 45 minutes.

Make 2 cuts halfway down each fig from the stem end to make cross-shaped incisions in their tops. Press the figs gently in their middles to open up the tops. Place on a plate, cover with film and chill for 45 minutes.

Remove the mint from the lime juice and discard, and add a pinch of salt to the juice. Gradually whisk in the crème fraîche, stirring constantly. Adjust the seasoning, if necessary.

Flood the base of 6 plates with the crème fraîche dressing. Arrange 3 figs decoratively on that. Arrange the ham strips and the salad leaves around them, garnish with the mint sprigs and serve immediately.

CAKES, PUDDINGS AND SWEETS

Many cooks tend to overlook the diversity of potential sweet uses of herbs. A whole range of readily available leaves, including mint, lemon balm and sweet cicely, and flowers, including lavender, geranium, marigold and elder, make the most delightful accompaniments to a wide variety of summer fruits. Sweet dishes based on dairy products – such as custards, fools and cheesecakes – are good candidates for flavouring with herbs, especially elderflowers, rose petals, lemon balm and bay. Some herbs like rosemary, geranium leaves, poppy seeds and aniseed work particularly well in baked dishes such as cakes, sponges and biscuits, as do the candied leaves and stems such as angelica.

Left: Pear Griestorte with Almonds and Ginger (page 56); centre: Spiced Oranges with Lavender and Pine Nuts (page 57)

PEAR GRIESTORTE WITH ALMONDS AND GINGER

SERVES 12–16

6 eggs, separated
225 g/8 oz caster sugar, plus more for dusting
juice and grated zest of 1 unwaxed lemon
115 g/4 oz fine semolina
30 g/1 oz ground almonds
30 g/1 oz ground ginger
3 drops of vanilla essence
6 ripe dessert pears, peeled and sliced
450 ml/¾ pt double cream, whipped to soft peaks
sprigs of mint, to decorate
butter, for greasing
flour, for dusting
icing sugar, for dusting (optional)

Preheat the oven to 180C/350F/gas4.

Grease two 20 cm/8 in diameter cake tins with butter and line their bases with discs of greaseproof paper (this is unnecessary if using non stick pans). Butter the greaseproof paper and then dust them and the sides of the pans with flour followed by caster sugar.

In a large bowl, beat the egg yolks and sugar together until pale, creamy and light. Add the lemon juice and continue beating until the mixture thickens. Stir in the semolina, almonds ginger and lemon zest and mix thoroughly. Whisk the egg whites to stiff peaks and gently fold them into the mixture.

Spoon into the prepared tins and cook for 30–40 minutes. The mixture will rise dramatically owing to the proportion of egg to starch. Do not open the oven or the mixture will subside!

Allow the cakes to cool, then split them across horizontally. Stir the vanilla essence and some of the pear slices into the whipped cream. Sandwich all the sponge layers together with this mixture and then top with the remaining pear slices. Dust with extra icing sugar, if wished, and decorate with mint.

If preferred, the traditional Austrian gâteau GRIESTORTE *may be made as two smaller cakes rather than one big one as described here.*

SPICED ORANGES WITH LAVENDER AND PINE NUTS

4 large thin-skinned unwaxed oranges
2 tbsp unrefined cane sugar
¼ tsp ground cinnamon
¼ tsp ground cloves
1 level tbsp finely snipped lavender leaves
2 tbsp redcurrant jelly
2 level tbsp pine nuts, roasted

Peel the oranges with a potato peeler, reserving the rind of one. Cut the oranges into thin slices and arrange these on a dish.

Put 300 ml/½ pt of water in a pan over a moderate heat. Add the sugar, cinnamon and cloves and bring to the boil, stirring constantly to dissolve the sugar. Keep at a low but constant boil until the liquid thickens into a syrup.

Add the lavender leaves, then pour any juices that have drained from the oranges into the syrup. Add the redcurrant jelly and bring to the boil again.

Cut the orange rind into julienne strips, add these and boil for 3 minutes more.

Pour the syrup over the oranges, sprinkle with the toasted pine nuts and serve immediately.

MULBERRY ZABAGLIONE WITH EAU DE COLOGNE MINT*

3 tbsp fresh mulberries, puréed
½ tsp finely chopped eau de cologne mint leaves
1 tbsp Marsala
30 g/1 oz caster sugar
6 egg yolks, beaten
*(*see page 2 for advice on eggs)*

Sieve the mulberry purée and spoon it into 4 glasses.

Put the mint leaves in a small bowl and pour over the Marsala. Cover and leave to macerate for 1 hour at room temperature.

Place the caster sugar, egg yolks and the Marsala mixture in a double boiler over a pan of hot (not boiling) water. Keep at a moderate heat, beating constantly with a whisk or an electric hand beater, until the mixture becomes thick and creamy.

Pour over the purée and serve immediately.

ZABAGLIONE is a frothy Italian custard made from egg yolks beaten with sugar and alcohol. Usually served hot in tall glasses, it is most commonly flavoured with Marsala, but some versions use sparkling white wine or even liqueurs.

COULIS *is the French term for a thick sauce or purée, usually of fruit or vegetables.*

STAR ANISE *is a pungent star-shaped spice with a strong aniseed flavour. It is very popular in Chinese cooking and is a constituent in their much-used five-spice powder. It must be used with caution as it can drown the other flavours in a dish.*

PEACHES WITH CHESTNUT AND ROSEMARY PURÉE

2 tsp rosemary leaves
2 tbsp sweetened chestnut purée
115 g/4 oz fresh raspberries
4 large very ripe sweet peaches, halved, stoned and peeled
150 ml/¼ pt double cream, whipped to soft peaks
2 tbsp crushed pistachio nuts

Put the rosemary leaves in a coffee grinder or food processor and blend to a powder. Put this in a sieve and dust it into the chestnut purée. Blend it well into the purée.

Liquidize the raspberries in the blender or food processor and then push them through a fine sieve to make a raspberry coulis.

Flood the base of 4 chilled plates with the coulis and arrange 2 peach halves on each plate. Cover the peach halves with the chestnut purée, followed by the cream. Finish with the pistachio nuts and serve immediately.

SUMMER FRUITS WITH STAR ANISE AND BORAGE

SERVES 6

1 whole star anise
85 g/3 oz granulated sugar
thinly pared rind of 2 unwaxed oranges
150 ml/¼ pt light red wine
115 g/4 oz redcurrants
115 g/4 oz blackcurrants
115 g/4 oz raspberries
115 g/4 oz blackberries
285 g/10 oz strawberries, halved
10 borage flowers
crème fraîche, to serve

Place the star anise, sugar and orange rind in a pan with 150 ml/¼ pt of water and place over a gentle heat. Stir constantly, until the sugar dissolves. Then cook for 5 minutes.

Add the wine and bring to the boil. Boil for 3 minutes, then cover and simmer for 5 minutes. Remove from the heat and allow to cool. Remove the star anise from the syrup.

Place the fruit in the syrup and toss well to combine. Cover and chill for 24 hours.

Just before serving, chop some of the borage flowers and toss these thoroughly into the salad. Garnish with the remaining whole flowers and serve with crème fraîche.

Top: Summer Fruits with Star Anise and Borage; bottom: Peaches with Chestnut and Rosemary Purée

TREACLE TART WITH ORANGE THYME

SERVES 6

140 g/5 oz unsalted butter, cut into small pieces, plus more
for greasing
200 g/7 oz flour
1/2 tsp salt
4 egg yolks
7 tbsp fresh breadcrumbs, preferably a mixture of white and
brown
4 tbsp golden syrup
2 tbsp flaked almonds
2 tbsp grated zest and the juice from 1/2 unwaxed lemon
1 tbsp finely chopped orange-scented thyme leaves

Preheat the oven to 200C/400F/gas6 and grease a 24 cm/9½ in flan dish with butter.

Sift the flour with the salt into a bowl. Add the butter and rub it in with the fingertips until the mixture resembles breadcrumbs. Using a fork, mix the egg yolks in lightly, together with enough cold water to make a firm dough.

On a cold lightly floured surface, knead the dough for 2 minutes and then roll it out to a thickness of about 3 mm/⅛ in. Use it to line the prepared dish and prick the base gently with a fork.

Mix the remaining ingredients together and spread them evenly over the base. Use the pastry trimmings to decorate the top of the tart.

Bake for 25-30 minutes on the middle shelf of the oven, until golden. Serve hot, warm or cold.

Left: Apple Brown Betty with Scented Geranium right:
Treacle Tart with Orange Thyme

APPLE BROWN BETTY WITH SCENTED GERANIUM

SERVES 4–6

9 slices of stale brown bread, crusts removed
55 g/2 oz softened butter
900 g/2 lb cooking apples, peeled, cored and sliced
3 tbsp golden syrup
1 tbsp finely chopped scented geranium leaves
Greek yogurt, custard or cream, to serve

Preheat the oven to 160C/325F/gas3.

Spread the slices of bread generously with butter and cut each slice into quarters.

Place a layer of one-third of the bread quarters over the base of a pie dish. Cover this with half the apple, dribble one tablespoon of golden syrup over and then sprinkle over half of the geranium leaves.

Repeat with a second similar layer and finish with a layer of overlapping bread quarters to cover. Spread this with the remaining syrup.

Bake for 50 minutes, then increase the temperature to 190C/375F/gas5 and bake for 10 minutes more, until crisp and golden brown. Serve hot, warm or cold with yogurt, custard or cream.

MARIGOLD AND APRICOT SORBET*

SERVES 4–6

3 tbsp sugar
325 g/11 oz canned apricot halves in syrup, drained
1 egg white, whisked until stiff
*(*see page 2 for advice on eggs)*
juice of 1 lemon
petals from 2 marigold (calendula) heads

In a saucepan, dissolve the sugar in 150 ml/¼ pt water. Bring to the boil and cook until it is syrupy, stirring constantly. Allow to cool.

Purée the apricots in a blender or food processor, then strain this through a fine sieve. Stir in the egg white and lemon juice. Then mix this into the syrup.

Put the mixture into an ice-cream maker or in ice trays with half the marigold petals sprinkled into it. If using an ice-cream maker, follow the manufacturer's instructions; otherwise place the trays in the freezer until just set, whisking several times with a fork to disperse large crystals as it freezes.

Serve in chilled glass dishes, decorated with the remaining marigold petals.

PEPPERMINT CREAMS WITH FRESH MINT*

MAKES 24–36

225 g/8 oz icing sugar
1 egg white, beaten
*(*see page 2 for advice on eggs)*
½ tbsp finely chopped fresh mint
6 drops of peppermint essence

Sift the icing sugar into a bowl. Gradually add the egg white, stirring constantly until a stiff paste is formed.

Add the fresh mint and the peppermint essence and combine well. Lightly knead the mixture with the fingertips for 3 minutes.

On a cold surface, roll the paste out to a thickness of 6 mm/¼ in between two pieces of greaseproof paper.

Remove the top sheet of paper. Using a 2.5 cm/1 in round pastry cutter, stamp out the creams, re-rolling trimmings as necessary.

Allow to dry out for 24 hours before serving.

Always invest in the best-quality flavouring ESSENCES. *Inferior brands are usually synthetic and their flavour can mar a dish. Natural essences don't keep well, so buy only just as much as you need.*

GOOSEBERRY FOOL WITH ELDERFLOWERS

450 g/1 lb gooseberries
115 g/4 oz unrefined cane sugar
5 elderflower heads
1 level tbsp custard powder
1 level tbsp caster sugar
150 ml/¼ pt milk
150 ml/¼ pt double cream, lightly whipped
almond biscuits, to serve (optional)

Place the gooseberries in a pan with the cane sugar, 3 elderflower heads and 2 tablespoons of water. Cover and simmer until the fruit is completely soft. Remove from the heat and allow to cool.

Remove and discard 2 of the elderflower heads, then liquidize the mixture to a smooth purée and sieve it.

In a bowl, mix the custard powder and the caster sugar to a smooth paste with 2 tablespoons of the milk. Bring the rest of the milk to just below the boil in a saucepan and pour this into the custard paste, stirring constantly to blend. Return the custard to the heat and cook gently until it thickens. Allow to cool.

Fold the cream into the gooseberry purée, followed by the custard, combining them well. Chill thoroughly for 2 hours, before serving garnished with the remaining elderflowers and accompanied by almond biscuits, if using.

Left to right: Peppermint Creams with Fresh Mint (page 61), Marigold and Apricot Sorbet (page 61) and Gooseberry Fool with Elderflowers

ELDERFLOWERS
*have the useful
property of
neutralizing the
acidity of other
ingredients. It is for
this reason that they
are so popular with
sharp fruit, such as
rhubarb and citrus
fruits. Elderflowers
also have the
advantage of being
free to many of those
lucky enough to have
a tree growing in
their garden.*

INDEX

Page numbers in *italic*
refer to the photographs

ACKNOWLEDGEMENTS
The author would like to mention the following suppliers:

Jekka's Herb Farm,
Rose Cottage,
Shellards Lane,
Alveston, Bristol BS12 Y

Barrow Boar,
Fosters Farm,
North Barrow,
Yeovil, Somerset